IS YOUR THINKIN STINKIN?

"Change Your Thoughts, Change Your Life"

"When The Great God Let Loose
A Thinker On The Planet,
All Things Are At Risk"

Ralph Waldo Emerson

By Nnika Tinney

Wealth Strategist

Dedication

*To my little angels Kayla & Erica both of you
are reason I do what I do. It is my one desire to
infuse in you both with only Right thinking. You came
to this earth plane for a reason, this I know,
mommy wants you to soar.*

*To my parents you have inspired me in
more ways than one.*

*To all my siblings I hope that I have been a good
example to you all and that I continue to inspire each
one of you to pursue your dreams.
To my soul match you are truly magical. I love you.*

*To all my relatives and friends, and past co-workers I
hope that you find this book insightful and heartfelt.*

To the world at large, "let the DIVA in you Shine!"

What's In a Thought?

They say what you think about the most is what you bring about. I'm not sure who "They" are but, I have come to know there is much truth in this statement.

When I thought I was stupid I failed miserably on the test. When I thought I was smart I passed with flying colors and surpassed all the rest.

When I thought I was slow the other runners left me clear in the dusk. When I thought I was fast I jumped and reached beyond the blue sky.

When I thought I was pure, men with virtue only did I meet. When I thought I was loose they said to me, to you I will no longer speak.

When I thought I was poor to the welfare line I laid. When I thought I was rich my income doubled in a real estate niche.

When I thought I was ugly, no one did I adore. When I thought I was beautiful, in my life I did soared.

Whenever I thought of anything and emotionalized it did I realize in truth.

It is true my dear that whatever you think about the most is what you will bring about.

What have you thought about today?

Wealth Strategist

Appreciation

I give thanks to my parents, all three of them. Through the good and bad, the thick and thin you all have taught me lessons that have shaped me into the person I am today.

To all my siblings, I love you all. There were times when I wished I were the only child growing up. Now that I am all grown up I would not change any of our experiences together for nothing in the world.

To my two beautiful daughters, you two are the very reason; mommy strives every day to be a better person. Know that I am always thinking of the two of you and ensuring that I set a good example for you to reference to.

To all my family members, keep striving and look to the light for guidance and comfort.

I would like to thank all of my educators and teachers. I send my love to even the ones who doubted my abilities at times.

A special thank you to Mr. Ron Small, Ms. Sandra MacDonald and Coach Pierce, you guys pushed me and believed in me even when I didn't always believe in myself.

I would like to give a special thanks Ms. Alexis Herman, Robert Benjamin Johnson and the 1993 White House Staff for showing me the ropes, extending their warm words of encouragement and overall kindness during my internship. You all will never quite know or understand what your smiles and heartfelt words did for me back in those days.

I would also like to thank Former House of Representative Walter Tucker of Compton, Ca for taking the time out of your busy schedule back during my internship to allow me to interview you in order to complete my thesis. Many turned me down and claimed they were too busy to assist a struggling college student but not you. I don't care what others may say about you, Mr. Tucker you will always be all right with me.

I also like to thank my former employers and colleagues. You guys contributed to my personal and professional growth in more ways than I can count.

To many of the customers, clients and businesses that I worked with over the years I thank you for business, ideas, criticism and advice. For without you all, I would not have been able to afford the lifestyle I have grown accustomed to.

Special thanks go out to enlightened billionaires, millionaire mentors like Dr. Wayne Dryer, Jerry Clark,

Tony Robbins, Catherine Ponder, and Les Brown. Your books, audio programs, seminars and or television specials have taught me more than I ever learned in all the four and half years of college at UC Davis or the year and half at Bellevue University. I thank you all for having the courage to step up and live your lives on purpose and to be an expansion to the world.

Thank you, Stephanie & Barbara, my Spiritual Guidance and Life Coach. You are able to look into my soul and see the real me. Thank you for keeping it real with me and telling me like it is. The Great All loves you and so do I. Thank you Ms. Mary Thompson for referring me to Stephanie and for being a great friend.

There are many others, I could go on and on but then you'd never get to the meat of my book. So in case I have left anyone out please forgive. Just know that you are all very much appreciated.

TABLE OF CONTENTS

INTRODUCTION

Is your Thinkin Stinkin? You're probably wonder-ing what I mean by that statement. It's a term you might hear in my family at one of our holiday gather-ing or festivities. Have you found yourself engrossed in negative thoughts about someone or something that happened earlier that day or the night before or maybe even the week or months before? Or have you said to yourself, a coworker or supervisor doesn't even know it but they are one comment away from you going postal on them? Have you said to yourself "If my spouse, the kids, boyfriend or girlfriend say one more thing to me; I am going to reach out and touch them like AT&T?" Have you been driving down the street and had someone cut you off and you immediately started plotting out in your mind how you were going to hunt them down, run them off the road and set their car on fire? If you have answered yes to any of these possible scenarios, then your Thinkin is mostly definitely Stinkin.

You are probably wondering how can you change these negative thought patterns and are you normal. Well, I am here to tell you that you can change these types of thoughts to more positive ones and yes, you are normal. There have been many occasions when I perceived someone's behaviors or actions as totally ridiculous and asinine. I have actually gone postal myself, a few times in this lifetime; and I can't promise that I won't have a few more occasions to let loose. During those times, I didn't feel the most proud of myself. I am sure you will probably say the same. However, one thing that I have learned is that you can't beat yourself about the past. Actually it is ridiculous and insane to because the past is forever gone and future doesn't exist. All we have is the here and now, the gift of the present. And if that is true, why then do so many of us exert so much time and energy consuming ourselves with negative thoughts that do not serve or preserve the gift of life in the NOW? These are some of things that I would like to explore in this book.

This book is by no means the all to end of all on this subject. However, it is my intention to offer you some insight through my experiences and people that I have come across thus far on my journey as to why and how we think the way we do and why we get the results that we do. I hope to expand your thinking just a little bit. I hope that I get you to laugh just a little bit. I hope I get you to see yourself a little bit differently by the end of this book. It is my belief and true desires that if I am able to accomplish this, then I have managed to make a difference in the world through you, my reader. One of my favorite quotes that I heard Dr. Wayne Dryer say is "When you change the Way you look at things, then the things you look at will change." I love this quote so much because it reminds me that change starts from the inside. But how can you change your thinking if you are not even aware of whether or not it is Stinkin? Hence, the idea of this book came about to me. This book may at times seem like an autobiography because in different parts I will share with you pieces of my personal journey. However, this book is not an autobiography in totality. Some of the stories may not be an exact rendition of what happened but I did my best to recall all the details. I would love to hear from anyone who can relate to some of the ideals and stories in this book. I know that I am not alone. Share, love, give, and receive all that you are as I do the same.

Nnika Tinney

Wealth Strategist, Author, Speaker, Entrepreneur

CHAPTER ONE

Wake Up Pissed Off

Have you ever woke up with television still on and you're upset but not really sure why? The alarm clock goes off loudly, you hit it and slowly arise from the comforts of your warm bed and soft pillow saying to yourself and "It's Monday and today is going to be a long day." If you're like most people you're already thinking about Friday and hoping the week goes by as fast as possible, so that you can get to the weekend. After you finish all your grooming you rush out the door perhaps with a cup coffee in your hand just in time to hit the morning traffic. As you're fighting your way through traffic to get to the office, another driver is not paying attention and almost hits your car. You become so enraged that you tailgate the guy and give him the middle finger, further reminding him how incompetent of a driver he really is.

On the radio, they remind you about all the accidents that have taken place throughout the city that morning. You finally make it to the office just to discover that the parking lot is nearly full and you have to park in the back, making your walk to the front door of the office take a few extra minutes that feel more like a few extra hours. You get to your desk and a co-worker comes over because he feels it's his duty to barf on you about how bad his weekend was or about the latest gossip in the office, the latest drama with Iraq or whatever bad news he could think of. By the time you get started with some actual work it's almost lunchtime, and you haven't accomplished half the things on your list. You are irritable, and dreading coming back into the office after lunch because you know your manager is going to ask you if you have completed the such and such project yet. You say to yourself, "If he asks me that one more time, I am going to scream."

First Tip to Clearing Stinkin Thinkin

Ok stop right there! Do you see what's happening here? Let's back track on how the day started. Better yet, let's go back to Sunday night. You fell asleep with the television on. This is a **BIG mistake #1.** I know some of you may not agree with me on this one. I have one girlfriend who swears she has to have the TV on in order to go to sleep. I wonder what she would have done had she been born prior to when televisions were invented. Perhaps she would count sheep? Incidentally this girlfriend has severe road rage practically every time she gets in her car. Once she even got into a physical confrontation on the side of the highway with another woman over a traffic infraction. Most of us have no idea the power of subliminal messages passed through the television that seeps into our subconscious mind while we are awake less known asleep. If you have gotten into the habit of sleeping with the television on, you must and I repeat you **MUST**, stop this habit immediately. It is a matter of life and death!

There are two aspects to your mind, your conscious mind and your subconscious mind. Your subconscious mind cannot distinguish between good or bad, right or wrong. It doesn't know when you are joking. It just soaks up everything that it hears internally and externally up like sponge. Why take the chance that something negative or not for your best good, could get in while you're sleeping. I know from personal experience that falling asleep with the television on can be damaging to one's subconscious mind firsthand.

The Second Tip to Clearing Stinkin Thinkin

Not falling asleep with the television is a great first step in the right direction. I know for some of you like my girlfriend, this is a tall order but I promise you won't regret it. I use to love to watch the popular TV show "Law and Order." I could watch episode after episode. I would discover later on in my journey to mental cleansing why I had a lot of bad dreams that would wake me up during the night. I once heard my mentor, Master Trainer Jerry Clark (Clubrhino.net), say, "Though is not impossible to shift your thinking on your own, sometimes it is more challenging because we can't always get a clear picture when we are standing in the frame." I would tend to agree with him on that one. Whether you enlist my services (see www.west-coast-media-solutions.com) or someone else's, do yourself a favor and invest in a personal development coach. This was one of the first things I did after attending an Anthony Robbins' seminar on developing the Power Within.

The Third Tip a 30-Day Mental Fast

I had no idea what I was in store for with hiring a coach. I mentioned to my coach that sometimes I woke up angry and irritated but I wasn't always sure of why. One of the first things my coach asked me was to describe to him what I did in the evening before going to bed and when I arose in the morning. I wasn't quite prepared for what my coach would have me do next. A 30-day Mental Fast was in order he said, which meant I was to stop watching TV for 30 days among other things. I never considered myself a big television watcher, but I did have my favorite shows like Law and Order and CSI. He told me that it would make a huge difference in how I thought about my day and myself. He said you have to watch what goes in your mind with the same tenacity, as a top athlete would watch what goes into her body. He promised me that I wouldn't miss anything and that I would see a huge difference in my attitude and in my dreams. Guess what folks? He was right. It was a little difficult at first. Eventually, the nightmares stopped completely.

The Fourth Tip- Do Sometime Else With Your Time

Instead of watching TV at night or in the morning, I occupied myself with reading inspirational and self-improvement books. I would also play a soft meditation program, which relaxed me, and this would aide me in falling asleep. Most nights I slept like a baby.

The Fifth Tip- Do Away With That Alarm Clock

The next item I want to address in regards to how the day started in this scenario is the alarm clock. Have you ever thought about how you feel when you are in a deep sleep and suddenly awakened by your alarm clock? I never really gave it much thought myself. Although I did realize that I began to have this love hate relationship with my alarm clock. Isn't it funny how on Saturday mornings we never seem to have a problem with waking up early? Or let Monday be a national holiday of some sort and we can pop up bright and early at 6:00 am with no alarm clock at all. But let it be a workday and boy oh boy, you couldn't pay most of us to get up at 6:00 am without our trusty alarm clock.

Somehow, we have managed to condition ourselves in believing that we can't wake up in time for work without an alarm clock sounding off in our ears. Doing away with an alarm clock or at least setting it to soft relaxing music was another suggestion given by my life coach. I took him up on it and amazingly enough, I began to feel so much better upon rising out of bed. After a while, I no longer needed to use an alarm clock at all. You see just as we condition our minds to swim, ride a bike, learn to read and write; you can condition your mind to wake your body at any appropriate time necessary for you to conduct your day. It first starts with you suggesting to yourself that you want to and plan to make a change. It was simply a habit to use an alarm clock. And just like you made that a habit you can unmake it. You must begin with recognizing that your prior act was just habit, which began with an idea that turned into a thought and that thought turned into an action, which when repeated, became a habit.

When the day came that I was no longer a hostage to my alarm clock, I shouted out the old spiritual "Free at last, Free at last, Thank God Almighty I am free at last". Now if there is a power outage or whatever I don't concern myself with such matters. Of course, you must recognize that if you do oversleep there is no one or thing to blame anymore but yourself. That might be a scary thought to some but to me it is truly liberating. Why? It is the first step to the realization that I am in control of my destiny and me. No one or, nothing, not even an alarm clock can control my biological clock.

What about getting out of the habit of thinking Mondays are always bad days or long days? I have often wondered, "Where did that thought originate from?" I am sure those folks that passed on to the next life with their music (life purpose) still in them would say, "Any day and every day that we have an opportunity to expand the universe with our true-life expression is a GREAT day." Remember in our story, here we told ourselves that it was Monday and that it was going to be long day.

Have you ever left the house and said today is going to be a great day and it turned out to be just that? Have you ever said to yourself "I am going to close that deal today" or "I know someone is going to call me with great news" and it happened? Many folks would say that this was just pure coincidence. But those of us who are aware of the universal law of attraction know that, "That which is like itself is drawn unto itself." To put it in plain old English, what you think about most is what you bring about. If you think and speak with words that Mondays suck and then in all likelihood Mondays will suck for you. There is an old saying that has been passed down from generation to generation that goes something like this "Be careful what you ask for because you just might get it." Well, I say "Know what it is that you ask for because you most certainly will get it, the universe doesn't discriminate."

Think of it this way, your subconscious mind is on the job 24-7 building your body, recreating and regenerating your cells so that your body can function. Every time you have continuous negative thoughts; every time you sow seeds of pessimism into your mind; every time you chose to have thoughts of jealousy, worry, fear, doubt or lack; you damage and destroy your vital organs. You literally think yourself sick and you open yourself up to the possibility of infections. You create with your thoughts a body at dis-ease (disease). It's not normal to think Mondays suck. Have you ever seen a little kid running around on a Monday saying, "It's Monday and today sucks"? Probably not, that type of negative thinking and self-talk is something many us developed over time. It's a habit and like I mentioned before, it's a habit that we can break by simply changing our thoughts, which in turn change our words.

The Sixth Tip- Try Positive Affirmations

A good affirmation to state to yourself or even write it down on a post-it note somewhere in your home where you can see it on Sunday night and Monday morning might be something like *"I love and appreciate Monday mornings, for today is a gift from the Creator and a chance for me to expand the Universe with my many talents and gifts."* If you say that often enough with conviction and feeling, eventually you will find yourself looking forward to Mondays. If that doesn't work, then you might want to re-examine your chosen profession. There is no point in dedicating over half of your adult life to something that you don't enjoy. I'm sure the last thing you want your obituary to say is "Tameka worked at XYZ Company for 40 yrs or Tameka had her own business for 40 yrs doing such and such and she hated every minute of it!" I think I can honestly say that deep down inside we all want to feel like we made a difference in this world and that somehow because of us, the next generation will have a better more prosperous life because we were here.

The Last Tip on Changing How You Feel When You Wake-up

Waking up in a state of anger is also a sign that you are more than likely not working in a profession that is your life calling. People who are living life on their terms and doing what they love look forward to not only Mondays, but they look to forward to everyday. That is not to say that they don't have unpleasant experiences. The trick is to flip the dial tune switch in your head when things appear bleak to the learning station. In other words, ask yourself what am I to learn from this situation and why am I feeling this way. This level of introspection takes courage and practice. Whether we want to admit it or not, as human beings, we thrive on challenges and adversity.

Think about whenever you have set a goal and through focus and right action and you achieved it, you felt invigorated and alive. Conversely, whenever you gained something for nothing you didn't receive the same level of satisfaction. Men provide women, and women provide men the classic example of our yearning for challenges and adversity and why they are so necessary. Just think about the times when you had a man or a woman pursue you. Wasn't the true thrill in the unknown and the fun in the pursuit or was it in the obtaining of your desires? It was in the pursuit of course! This is why ladies, once we give in and say "I DO" the majority of men stop doing many of things they did when they were trying to secure our love and affection. One of things that I like to do for my love interest and me is to change my hairstyle on a consistent basis. At least that way, he gets the impression of a new woman every other month. (smile)

CHAPTER TWO

Rage-aholics

Our world has become one where everything has to be done now. There is no time or space for slackers. Many folks are operating in the mode of; "I have to eat you before you eat me." I have to admit I have been guilty a time or two of giving someone the middle finger while driving. By no means do I write this book and profess to be an angel. I have had my moments where I have lashed out. You know those times when we have told ourselves that we have to get downright UGLY and show that part of our self that is less than intelligent. However, have you ever stopped to think how childish, immature and potentially dangerous it is to tailgate someone and pull up beside them to curse them out for a traffic infraction?

I can recall ten or eleven years ago my parents were going on their very first vacation together in a number of years. My Mom was so excited because they were taking a trip to the Bahamas and would be staying at a nice resort. They asked me to drive them to the airport in Sacramento so that they would not have to leave their car there, for a week while on vacation. I agreed and picked them up from their home in Stockton, Ca. On our way to the airport while driving on the freeway, I accidentally crossed lanes and didn't see a car in my blind spot. Fortunately, we didn't collide and all was well or so I thought. The driver of that car wasn't so forgiving. He began to tailgate me. I switched lanes again to allow him to move ahead but that didn't work. He switched lanes to get behind me so that he could continue to tailgate me. This continued for miles until a highway patrol was spotted and then the other driver stopped temporarily. My father insisted that I get behind the car and do to him what he had been doing to us. For reasons I can't explain even to this day, I followed my dad's orders.

Low and behold the other car was on their way to the airport as well. We finally arrived at the airport and my dad insisted that we park right alongside of this driver. So I did. Before I could park correctly my father jumped out of the car and rushed up to the driver and out comes several teenagers. They looked terrified. My dad proceeded to curse them out, and tell them that if it weren't for the fact that he was going on vacation, he would beat all of their asses! Looking back on this incident now, I realize how careless it was on my part to follow my dad's demands. This incident could have turned into a nightmare for all of us. Our lives could have been altered forever in way in which we would have regretted. My father has deep-seated anger and emotional issues; I suppose at the time I did too or otherwise I would have listened to my own soul and not listened to him at the time.

Most of us that have admitted we've participated in such negative activities like this, failed to realize that the very act of this set a cause in motion, which produces disastrous results. In some instances, events like this will lead up to prison time, financial losses and in some cases murder. For what purpose do we do these types of things? One may argue that the other person's action made you react this way. Famous motivational speaker Les Brown says, "It doesn't matter what happened to you or around you, it's what happens in YOU that counts." So let's get one thing perfectly clear, no one makes us act any certain way.

Everything we do or don't do is a choice. There is absolutely nothing in this world that we have to do. I challenge anyone who can present to me something that is an absolute must. Now does that mean if we don't do certain things like; brush our teeth, pay the rent or mortgage, car note etc. that there won't be consequences? There will be, but when it's all said and done we do have a choice in everything that we do or think. You can choose to REACT or you can choose to RESPOND. When you respond, you take your ego out of it and you learn to operate from your Higher Self (or the God within). When you operate from your Higher Self, you are then able to come from Love. Just about any religious doctrine in the world in one form or another will tell you that *Love conquers all.* I am learning to send love to my fellow commuters vs. the middle finger. Doing this has done wonders for my attitude and I am convinced it will do wonders for yours as well.

I use to think that it was other people's stupidity that made me angry. I have since realized that people don't make me angry. I chose to be angry and upset. I chose to respond with anger. Let me say this, anger isn't always a bad thing. Sometimes it's appropriate to be angry. Sometimes it's not only appropriate to confront someone whom you feel has wronged you but it is downright necessary. The trick is to come from love and your peace, address the issue and then let it go. If you don't do this you will find yourself filled with resentment. And resentment more often times than not, will eventually lead you to a body at dis-ease. If you or someone you know is constantly suffering from one aliment or another, chances are very high that you or this individual are harboring a lot of anger and resentment. Release the anger and resentment and you can literally perform a physical healing in your body.

I am not exempt; I have held onto anger and frustration about things that have happened at work. When I did, I would get a sharp pain in my head and around my eyes. I would literally bring on a headache just by marinating in my anger. Now based upon my upbringing, marinating in my anger wasn't enough. I had to express it to whomever I felt was the root cause. I remember about five or six years ago things had gotten very busy at work, so busy in fact that management finally took action to hire additionally employees. As things would have it, a colleague and I finally got a much-needed assistant to share that was to help us with our workload. The individual that ended up being my assistant was a tall, 6'5", nicely built, caramel complexion brother. We will call him Raymond to protect his privacy. Raymond by all appearance came across as confident, smart and a go-getter. He made it clear to everyone that he had no intentions on staying in the role of assistance for long, and that he had his sites on bigger and better things like moving up to a sales consultant position. I admired his boldness. It reminded me of myself. My colleague and I set out to assist him in any way that we could by teaching him everything that we knew. As it turns out, Raymond was mostly all talk and little action. His work was incomplete and sloppy. He called in excessively with one excuse or another. Half the day, he stayed on the company phone making personal calls, surfing the Internet looking at Internet porn or sleeping at his desk. I allowed myself to become completely irritated by his behavior.

Then one day, I approached him about following up on project. He insisted that he did follow-up and take the appropriate actions necessary to move the project along. I verified with the individuals that he claimed to have called just to be told that they had not spoken to him or received any messages from him regarding the project. When I questioned him about this, an argument ensued. Before I knew it, both our voices had escalated into screams and shouts. Raymond was sitting down when I initially approached him. But once things became heated, he stood up and flexed him physical strength by pushing out his chest. I am sure I had at least one hand on my hip and one finger pointed up at him. Raymond then challenged me to take matters outside and handle it "man to man." Now I want you to keep in mind, I am 5'3 and ½ inches tall and he was 6'5". He towered over me but I was un-moved by his height because I had allowed my anger to consume me. I foolishly accepted his challenge. Luckily, a co-worker stepped in and escorted us both to the district manager's office. He was removed from the assistant role and eventfully terminated due to poor job performance. You see, we don't get angry we do anger. What I mean by that is we express anger in our bodies and throughout our cells. In some ways, many times we get a rush from getting angry. If you do anger often enough, your body will become addict-ed to the sensations that anger provides. After a while, you will find yourself angry most of the time and you won't even be conscientious of why. Hello world, my name is Nnika and I am a recovering rage-aholic! Take note my dear friends, the first step to recovery is admitting you have a challenge to overcome.

I once had a girlfriend tell me about a dear relative suffering needlessly because she insists on holding onto anger, hurt, and resentment for her ex-husband. They were married for many years until she discovered he had begun cheating on her with women on the Internet. He has since moved on with his life and over ten years later, she still gets a knot in her stomach anytime someone mentions his name. She refuses to see what part she played in the downfall of their marriage. As far as she is concerned, she was a good wife and everything was his entire fault. Now I am not saying he was right in doing what he did. However, I do realize that whenever there is a break down in a relationship both parties brought their own special drama to the dance. At least, I know this to be true in my own life. Every relationship that I have had that ended on what most would consider a "bad note" was due to the fact that I brought my own bag of drama into the mix. Sadly, this relative's health over this same period of time has slowly begun to disintegrate with one aliment after another.

Have you ever started what you thought was an innocent conversation with someone, and before you realized it the person was yelling at you, all because you said "How's the weather today?" I can recall going out on a date with a guy, and as we were sipping on our cocktails, getting to know each other, it suddenly occurred to me that this guy was literally yelling his words at me. When we departed, I felt like I just been in a verbal wrestling match. When I asked him why was he so angry and so serious about everything, he looked at me as if I was mentally retarded and said strongly, "I am NOT angry and if all I did was crack jokes, women or people in general wouldn't take me serious. Furthermore, I don't have time for games. So if you want to be my woman and pursue a relationship with me, then you had better let me know now!" I replied to him that I wasn't in a position to make such a decision at this time, and that I was keeping my options open. At the time I didn't realize that this probably wasn't the best thing to say to an angry person because he then replied, "I don't believe in being AN option to anyone, and you can just eliminate me from your list." My response to that was "Not a problem, consider it done." Obviously, he was totally clueless. I thought to myself boy oh boy, that man has got some anger and control issues! He called me for months after this incident insisting on exploring a future together.

Anger and rage are very strong emotions that we learn growing up. If you were bought up in an angry, argumentative, and unloving household; your chances increase of becoming an angry adult. My father is a rage alcoholic and proud of it. His words and tone were the most frightening. I remember urinating on myself on several occasions just from him raising his voice at me. Many of our behaviors and reactions we picked from loved ones. However, part of our evolution and growth involves forgiving our caretakers and recognizing that they did the best they knew how at the time. Remember holding on to past pains, having resentment toward others or blame doesn't hurt anyone but the person who is constantly angry.

Silent Rage

Are you one of those individuals who hold your anger in? You know the type of person that when you ask them are they upset they say, "No, nothing's wrong, I am perfectly ok." Their body language and energy is saying totally the opposite. Just because you don't say anything doesn't make you any less enraged then a verbally outspoken person. I believe that not verbally expressing your concerns is often times worse than holding it in. You can wreak havoc on your body when you hold in your frustration in this way as well. And just because you don't say anything doesn't make you any less of a control freak than the outspoken person. Remember folks, we don't get angry we DO anger.

Not confronting someone who you feel has been a catalyst in your anger doesn't make you a saint, nor does it do anything beneficial for the other person. After all, no one is a mind reader. Well, at least most of us are not. It is not someone else's responsibility to know if you are bothered by an event or situation. If you don't like what someone has said or did and you believe in your heart that they could potentially cause real damage to either you or someone; then it is your duty to speak up.

One of things a previous lover use to do that would irritate me to no end, was give me the cold shoulder when something was bugging him. Then when he finally couldn't stand it anymore weeks or months later, he would tell me how he didn't appreciate when I said so and so and I did such and such. By then I had forgotten all about the incident or simply didn't recall the situation in any detail. If you want peace and understanding, you have to speak up and voice your concerns. It's not fair to the other person for to you to holdback your feelings even if it turns out later they were misguided or misdirected.

Express or Not to Express, that is the Question

Often times if we were ignored, abused or told "Children are seen and not heard"; we tend to grow up thinking that it's best not to say how we really feel. For most of my childhood, I was told that I didn't have an opinion. That whatever my parents said was law, and that was the end of it. I told myself often that once I became an adult, I would never allow anyone to silence me again. Eighteen was my magic number. As I have gotten older, I have gotten bolder. I have no problem now with letting people know what's exactly on my mind. I think the older you get the less you care about the opinions of other people.

We can over do this as well. I have been told on several occasions that I can be too forward and blunt. My goal is to obtain balance. This is why I am always striving to self-improve. I understand many people are told similar things growing up. In most cases, you will either buck this idea or use everyone you come into contact as a sounding board for your opinions and attitudes.

Are you reclusive and introverted? Whichever way you are, you most certainly can trace it back to something that was either said to you repeatedly or done to you. The key is to trace back in your mind what specific instance(s) that first evoked this reaction out of you. Once you do that, then you can rewrite the script. Rewriting your script is not as difficult or daunting as it may sound. I will discuss more about rewriting the script or your past in chapter four.

CHAPTER THREE

Blame-olgoy

Do you suffer from this syndrome or know someone that does? If you do, you are not alone. A large portion of the American population does also. Many of us are accustomed to blaming someone else for many of the challenges and obstacles in life. It seems to be the American way these days. I must say it is certainly much more convenient to blame someone else than to take full responsibility for our own lives and circumstances. However, the truth of the matter is that each one of us has total control over how we chose to respond to life's curve balls.

Yeah, But What About the Ism's of the World?

There are some people in this world who insist on maintaining the status quo. Do racism, sexism, and other lower thought vibrations exist? Yes they do. I have had people ask me this question time and time again. And my response is the same, "Just because they exist for others, doesn't mean they have to exist for me in my mind."

I wonder if the people who say other groups are victimizing them, stopped proclaiming the victim role and instead come from a position of strength and equality; how would the opposing group respond? If we continue to hold onto these ideas of inequality, both from a victim standpoint, or perpetrator standpoint; the issue will continue to exist. In order for things to change, at least one side has to stand up and say "Enough is enough. Let's drop the drama now! We all come from the One Source of Light and no one culture, religion or beliefs is any greater or better than another!"

Think about how each one of us fought to get here. I mean you beat out approximately 200 to 300 million other spermatozoids to get here. Most of your competition died along the way and didn't even have a fighting chance. But you, the ultimate, unique and determined one; won against perhaps some of the greatest odds there were just to be here! You could have given up like the rest of them but you didn't. And why, because you intended to be here; you chose to be here. Hence, you are responsible for your life in totality. If you are not living your dreams whatever they might be, you have the power to change that. Forget about what people said to you growing up or what someone just said to you yesterday. You came into this dimension a winner! Your very existence already proves that. You are already somebody! You have a purpose and unique gift that you are supposed to share and expand. The question is when are you going to start living it, and stop blaming others for your decision to live a mediocre life?

Beliefs

Every situation, challenge, setback, or success can be directly linked backed to our belief system. Your life is the way it is right now good or bad because of the beliefs you held or currently still hold. But what is a belief? It is my opinion that a belief is nothing more than a stream of thoughts that you kept having over and over again; combined with a strong set of emotions tied to them. Certainly you have the right to believe in whatever you want. That's the beauty of the Universe! We all come here with a free will. We can choose to accept beliefs past down from our parents, friends, government, teachers etc. Whatever we choose to accept or reject our experiences is directly tied into our belief system. With that being said, why then do we continue to hold onto beliefs that no longer serve our highest good?

The single most likely answer to that is FEAR. Many of us fear the unknown even though we may know consciously that a situation; person or place no longer serves us. We will often time stick with it strictly out of familiarity. Haven't you heard people say or perhaps you've said it yourself, "I'd rather stick with the devil I know, versus exploring something new and take the chance of ending up in a worse situation." Because of past conditioning, we often think of a worse outcome versus the real possibility that a better opportunity is waiting for us just around the corner, if only we demonstrated just a little faith.

One of the ten secrets to Inner peace and success according the Dr. Wayne Dwyer is having a mind that is open to everything and attached to nothing. That does not mean that you have to accept everything, every idea or thought as your own. But also, it doesn't mean that you automatically reject every thought or idea that you are presented with either. Have you ever sat down and asked yourself, "Are my beliefs really mine? Or are they just a compilation of ideas and thoughts that have been passed down to me by my parents and others I have grown up around?"

I sat down a few years ago and asked myself this very question. I really wanted to know, "Did I have the religious beliefs that I held so dearly because I truly felt them in my heart or was I just repeating what I have been conditioned to accept as a child growing up?" I discovered that I really didn't believe half the things that I had been taught growing up as child, and that I was in fact more connected to people of other faiths in more ways than one. Since I have opened myself up to have a more accepting attitude about people who have different ideologies than me, I have experienced tremendously more joy in my life.

I no longer feel the need to be right or to prove someone else's religious beliefs are wrong. Not being attached to a particular religion is so liberating! Coming to the realization that I am a spiritual being having a human experience has truly set me free. You see it is in our attachments to our beliefs that no longer serve us, just like the desire to control someone or something. It is the holding on to these attachments that you find where your Thinkin is stinkin the most.

Wars have been started and many human lives wasted behind dogmatic beliefs. Isn't it about time we entertain the concept of oneness? I mean would you really care what a person's beliefs was if you needed a lifesaving organ transplant? Or perhaps a close family member needed one, like one of your children or your parents? Would you care about a person's religious belief then? I think not. You know I find it quite entertaining how sometimes people have convenient religious beliefs.

A funny thing happened to a former business partner of mines once. We were at a book signing event when my former business partner saw a young woman passing our booth. He approached her and asked her if she would be interested in purchasing a signed autographed copy of his book She replied, "What's your book about, because I'm a ------------ and I don't just go around reading anything." She further asked, "What's your religious affiliation?" She followed that statement up with, "You must know how to do something right because most women don't like short men or men that are the same height as them." First off we both found these statements very odd considering his book clearly said it was about his awakening experience and self-esteem. My former partner responded and asked, "What does my personal beliefs have to do with whether you decide to purchase my book or not. Especially when it clearly states that it is speaking on the topic of self-esteem and it's apparent to me that based on your comments, you deserve to purchase a copy of my book more than anyone else." He then sealed it with this statement, "It is not that I am too short, it's that your vision isn't tall enough yet." Her jaw dropped and her publicist nodded in agreement. She suddenly saw the error in her statements and said, "You're right, I will take a copy of your book and by the way, I would like to give you a copy of my latest music CD." I wondered after that episode if she went around to every merchant that she patronized and asked him or her, what his or her beliefs were before she would buy anything. Somehow I doubt she did that. I call what she had, was selective religion. I think a lot of people suffer from this dis-ease of the mind.

Since I make this a point in my book, you have probably guessed that I also suffered from this dis-ease of the mind at one point in my life. I was raised up in the Baptist Christian Church. Up until I went off to college. In my third year, I had never bothered to study and learn about other religious beliefs. It was not something that was encouraged in my family. Actually if someone believed in anything different than Baptist Christian philosophy, it was pretty much assumed that you were utterly confused and most likely going to hell. I was very dogmatic in my beliefs at one point in my life.

I remember in my sophomore year, I was speaking to a dear friend of mine on the phone about the Christian faith. I don't recall word for word the conversation or how it even came about, but we began to argue about how God viewed gays. I insisted that homosexuality was a sin in the eyes of the church, and in the eyes of God, and that anyone practicing homosexuality was condemned to hell for eternity, unless they repented. My friend wept on the phone and we hung up both feeling angry and hurt. Our relationship was never the same after that. For many years, this person refused to speak to me or come around. I later heard thru the gossip channel that this same individual had confided in another individual that they had been molested as a child and was secretly living a gay lifestyle. I have since dropped my dogmatic views and I realized that this person was hurting and was trying to open up to me about some deep emotional pains, but I let them down because I was being judgmental and short sided. We have spoken in recent years and I believe that they have forgiven me. I learned a very valuable lesson from that experience. You never really know what someone has been through or what he or she is going through and showing a little compassion can go a long way.

I have also come to know that hell isn't some place that people go to when they pass away. Hell (in my opinion) is the mental picture we create in our own minds while we are living. It is not my place to tell anyone what their internal Creator has in store for their soul, whether in this life or the afterlife. What someone chooses to do and with whom they choose to do it, within the privacy of their own bedroom, is their concern. If the two individuals are consenting people of sound mind, who are we to say what they should or should not do? I know some folks are not going to like me saying this, but I am saying it anyway.

Number one, because it's my book. Secondly, because I feel too much time and energy is wasted debating over what two consenting individuals should or shouldn't be doing in the bedroom. Some things are just not our business!

CHAPTER FOUR

Drop the Drama

Have you ever heard the R&B singer Mary J. Blige soulful song, "No More Drama?" Many of us probably caught ourselves driving down the street singing that song until our hearts were content, but not really eternalizing the words and true meaning behind them. If you really listen to the words in that song, you would notice that Mary is singing about releasing attachments to people, places and things. When you see her and listen to her now, compared to 10 years ago, you know that she has done exactly what she sings about in that song. When are some of you going to decide to drop the drama and get on with your life?

As long as you hold onto the drama whether it is unhealthy relationships, unfulfilling jobs and careers, judgmental religious beliefs and doctrines, and superficial smiles; you won't be free. You will continue to live a life where you are constantly striving to survive or maintain to keep up with the Jones, but you will never quite arrive. You may be thinking, "Who the hell is she to tell me this?" Well let me say this, I am someone who chose to be born. So that I could beat the odds as a child of; poverty, domestic violence, drug and alcohol abuse by both parents and illiteracy (One parent barely surpassing grammar school and the other dropping out in the 11th grade).

Like some of you, I know what it is like to have nothing, to eat accept maybe some beans and maybe some rice, or noodles. I know what it's like to live in homeless shelters, or to have a parent say to you "Mama ain't got no money to buy you no school clothes right now. When my check comes on the 1st of the month, we will see if we can get you something."

I know what it's like to be a teenager and your parents not have a car, so you have to put your dirty clothes in a shopping cart and push the cart down the street to the local laundry mat to wash them. I know what it's like not have any money and have to wash your clothes in the bathtub. I know what it's like to walk into a room and see your mom or your dad high as the sky smoking a crack pipe! I know what it's like to wonder why in the hell your dad is constantly wearing long-sleeved shirts in the middle of summer with 110' degree weather. And then when you ask him why, he makes up some ridiculous lie and says, "Oh it's because I was feeling a little cold." But one day you see him coming out of the bedroom after taking a shower with no shirt on and you see the sores and fresh track marks on his arms and your heart drops into your stomach because you know that he wasn't wearing long-sleeve shirts in the middle of the summer because he was cold. He was wearing them to cover up the needle marks from the heroin he has been abusing his body with.

I know what it's like to come home and discover your favorite pair of pants or your walk-man radio that your own parent(s) stole or that an aunt bought you for Christmas in order to feed their drug habits. I know what it's like to be a child and have to be an adult all at once because your parent(s) are too busy getting high or being co-dependents so you have to be the one to take care of your younger siblings. I know what it's like to have a parent who swears after they get put behind bars for theft or assault and battery or driving under the influence etc. that they promise this going to be the last time you have to see them like that.

Believe me when I say I have lived it, tasted it, and feared all of this! This is I why I can tell you to DROP THE DRAMA!! You have the power to drop your past childhood tragedies that no longer serve you. I could easily hold on to all of these things and other events that happened in my life. If you think, (after reading this) that I had a terrible childhood, you would be mistaken! I have had some great times growing up as a child. You can rewrite your past. How do I rewrite my past you might be saying? Here are few simple techniques you can use to assist you in the rewriting of your past.

Rewrite Your Past

Step 1: Write down all the things you consider horrible in your life for at least 30 minutes straight. Don't think; just write whatever comes to mind. After 30 minutes of writing, I want you to stop writing.

Step 2: Look at what you wrote. Breathe as you look at it. Take deep long breathes, in and out. (This is very important! Do not criticize, condemn, nor speak ill of your past! Consider all the events that you are not fond of, or do not like as lessons to be learned from, even if you have not yet discovered the lesson. Finally, forgive and love everyone in this part of your past including yourself. Avoid making yourself wrong.) This is worth reading at least 21 times in a row!

Step 3: Whenever you think of anything that happened in step 1 of this exercise, smile at the thought and say, "I love you and I intend to learn your powerful message for a better life."

(Take the sheet of paper with the things that you wrote that were painful, horrible or undesirable in your past and rip it up or burn it and flush it down the toilet.)

Step 4: Take out another sheet of paper and write for 30 minutes all the good times you had as a kid.

Like when you received your favorite toy. Or when someone complimented you on something you did really well. Or recall the time when you got to go to the park or saw your favorite movie, and/or received money, or whatever favorable situation comes to mind.

Step 5: Stop and look at what you wrote. Breathe in and out as you look at it.

Step 6: Put these pieces of paper in a special place for safekeeping. Whenever you are feeling down or sad, go get these pieces of paper and re-read them. Imagine yourself as a little kid again.

You have just rewritten your past. Simple. See how quick and easy it can be? Anyone can do this! Believe me when I say this, "If you do this exercise and you do it with passion and feeling, you will feel differently about yourself and your childhood." You may need to do the exercise several times or reinforce it by enlisting the services of a life coach life like me. Either way, do whatever you feel you need to do so that you can drop the drama.

If I could bottle this "free feeling," and sell it in the open market, I would! This feeling of freeness is better than my greatest orgasm. Maybe having said that, it will be the encouragement you need to take action NOW!

A few years ago I was speaking at an engagement in San Francisco, Ca to a youth organization and a young man in the audience asked me if I regretted anything about my past or if there was one thing that I would change if I could. I replied to him "No." There once was a time in my life when I would have said yes like many of you probably would say. However in the last few years, I have really come to understand that my past served to create who I am today. Had I not been the product of drug addicted parents, had the experience of partly growing up in the welfare system, living in homeless shelters and so forth; I mostly likely would not have become the person that I am now. All of those things have served me well. They were the fuel for my engine of self-motivation, determination and tough mindedness.

When a manager at one time in my career threatened me with the possibility of losing my job if I did not conform to his way of thinking or doing things, I was able to look him straight in the face eye to eye and say, "I have lived in some pretty difficult situations and have personally witnessed and experienced poverty up close. I know how to not only survive but also thrive in most situations. Everything that I have accomplished to this point in my life is because of Greatness or God within me. So do what you feel you must do and I will do what I feel I must to do." His face became flushed and red. He had never had anyone respond like that to him.

He said, "But what about your children?" I responded, "My children have never wanted or gone without for anything. Their needs and most of their wants have always been met and I see no reason why I should begin to believe or except anything different!" Needless to say, he never felt the need to have that type of conversation with me again. I am sure he must have thought that I was either crazy or fearless. Either way, I think he got the message.

When you are able to drop the drama of your past and embrace all that you have experienced, you gain tremendous power. You are able to see that what you may be experiencing in the present isn't any worse or stronger than what you went through in the past. And since you are still here and able to read this book, your past didn't kill you physically or mentally.

CHAPTER FIVE

Watch Your Words

For the most of us, we have been told growing up as children that if we didn't have anything nice to say then don't say anything at all. Though we were told this on many occasions, this wise advice fell on deaf ears. Our own self-talk is probably the most damaging to our self-esteem and well-being. No one is probably harder on us than we are on ourselves. I know when it comes to myself I am harder on myself then anyone could ever be. Because we can be our own worse critics at times, it is vital that we watch our own internal dialogue.

Whatever we speak in thought and project out in words, sooner or later we manifest into our lives. Not to mention the fact that however you talk to yourself and treat yourself, others will follow suit. Have you ever thought and said to yourself, "Damn I sure look good in these jeans!" And then as you are walking down the street or in a store or wherever, someone made the same comment to you that you had been saying to yourself? You probably shrugged such incidents off as just idle chatter or flattery and nothing more. However, what you experienced in this situation was the power of creative thought. I can think of many instances where I experienced the power of creative thought. I absolutely love to indulge myself with pedicures, manicures, massages, back and neck adjustments. Yes ladies and gentlemen, I believe 100% in treating myself good. I have had some say, particularly men that "Boy you are high maintenance!" My Diva response to that was "If I don't show myself love and treat myself well, then I can't expect anyone else too!" I hope you caught that invaluable piece of wisdom that I just gave. Don't wait around for someone else to show you love and appreciation. You set the example and others will follow. Speaking of treating myself, I recall a few years ago I was walking around at the mall feeling good and refreshed because I had just treated myself to some new sandals and to French pedicure. I looked down to admire my feet and as I was looking at my feet I thought to myself "Girl you've got some sexy feet!" Just as I said this to my-self a young man was walking past me and said, "Yes girl your feet sure are sexy, in fact they are pretty enough to eat in my book!" I smiled, nodded and con-tinued on my way. At the time, it didn't occur to me that he had picked up on my internal dialog. He picked up on the conversation I was having with my-self.

Creative thought is actually the only real power. Biblical scriptures say, "In the beginning was the word and the word was with God and the word was God." If that be true, then thought and the spoken word is the only real power. In other words, your thought creates your words and your words create your reality. Therefore, your words have tremendous power. You see thoughts truly do travel. It's an illu-sion to think that our thoughts are private; we tele-path our thoughts, feelings, and words to others in si-lence, even we are not consciously aware of it. Be-cause the Great All is all knowing He or She knows that we humans have a challenge with knowing what we really want and so He gifted us with the buffer of time. We should really thank Him for that. Because if it was not for the time buffer, which gives us the op-portunity to really focus and emotionalize our true desires, we would constantly be undoing things, people and places that we manifested or spoke and thought into existence. Therefore, time really is on our side. Time is our friend and not our foe.

How do we change our words to be more encouraging and inspiring ones when we have been conditioned to use words that create lack, loss or limitation? We do it one day at a time. That's right. One day at a time. You were conditioned to use the words you are currently use one day at a time and it's going to take one day at a time to retrain your mind to use other more empowering words. You can speed the progress up by reading on a regular basis self-help books like this one, listening to motivational and inspirational audio programs, attending spiritual/breakthrough workshops among other things and hiring a Prosperity Coach like me. You could start each day by telling yourself how you want to and plan to feel for the day. These are just a few examples of the many wonderful things you could do that will make a huge difference in your vocabulary, thinking patterns and your life.

Will you have the occasion to slip up even after going through mounds of reprogramming? Yes, of course. However, the trick is that when you slip up don't beat yourself up about it. Tell yourself that it's ok and that you love yourself. Give yourself permission to not have the need or desire to be perfect all the time. It's not perfection to which we seek, but it's our intention behind our words and thoughts that are most important. Think about this, it is no different in the court system. If a person committed a crime, he or she will be more likely to get convicted and receive a harsher punishment if the jury felt or believed that their intent was more vicious or preplanned than if they had temporarily had a lapse in judgment. So even if you said, "I could kill him", when you become upset with your spouse or lover it doesn't mean that are you are forever condemned and have backslid into eternal damnation. If you keep saying things like that with emotion, energy and concentration; you will eventually attract a situation that can allow these words to become a reality. It is our emotions and our intent behind our words that create worlds. Therefore, we can use our words to create or we can use our words to destroy.

Have you ever taken a day and cataloged how many times you verbalized a negative word? Or maybe even thought a negative word? This is an excellent exercise that I would recommend for anyone. Maybe start by asking someone you trust and speak to often what disempowering words they hear you use most often. Then ask them if they would help you catalog how many times you use these words say in the course of a one-hour conversation with them. You will be surprised and amazed at how much of your time is wasted on using words that don't serve your higher good. You can also try this little exercise on other people that you talk to the most. You don't have to tell them you are doing it but just make a mental note of the number of times they too use disempowering words. You begin to see a pattern with the language that you use and the language that the people you associate with on regular basis. It has been said many times and in many ways that "Birds of a feather flock together."

When you embark upon the life long journey of self- improvement or self-development there is no turning back. Your accountability is higher to All There Is and therefore it is imperative that you change who you associate with on a regular basis to individuals who walk, talk and speak words of empowerment, joy, peace and prosperity. Your soul's livelihood depends on it. Having the understanding that I do now about the power of words, I asked myself where in the world did the childhood nursery rhyme of "Sticks and stones may break my bones, but words will never hurt me" come from? Sticks and stones may break a few bones but words can diminish as well as uplift our self-confidence and self-esteem.

My Cousin William's Story

I want to share with you the story of my cousin William Piggy. It's a powerful one and it stands out clearly in my mind right now as I write these words just how powerful our words and thoughts are. I met William when I was fifteen and he was thirteen. One of my uncles married his mother. Technically, we were not blood cousins but the minute I met William I took a liking to him and accepted him as a cousin. William was the type of person that was easy to like. He was easy going and friendly. He had a beautiful smile, a smooth coco colored complexion and at the time stood about 5'8" to 5'9". William had a gift for basketball. He was a natural. He admired Michael Jordan and would often try to emulate Michael's style of play. But unlike many kids that admired Jordan or played basketball, William wasn't obsessed by it or star struck. He wasn't the type of kid that insisted on playing basketball every day for hours. He didn't need to. It came natural to him like eating or breathing. He just kind of took it for what it was. By the time he entered high school, coaches were eying him. He played on the varsity team even though he was not an upper classmen. His coaches said he was a natural but they wished he would put forth more effort because he was a very promising future star. For whatever reason, only William really knows he was not interested in basketball in that way. He thought it was fun to play, but he didn't have a burning desire like Jordan or Magic Johnson that would propel him to pursue college or the pros for that matter. Regardless of natural abilities, if you don't have a burning desire or your thoughts are not in alignment with your actions, you will be ineffective.

William desires laid elsewhere. My uncle was a Baptist Preacher. Prior to William's mother marrying my uncle; they had lived a life of poverty, drugs and struggle. His mother was a recovering addict. Most of people William had been exposed to prior to meeting my uncle were either drug dealers or drug addicts. Some of his family members glorified the drug culture. Or at least that's the way William saw it. The fancy cars, fast money, women and lawless lifestyle impressed him. My uncle did his best to introduce William to a more positive environment. He lived in nice neighborhoods, received weekly allowances, received support for his basketball games and got nice name brand clothes and shoes. But still that wasn't enough to remove the twinkle from William's eyes regarding living the life of drug dealer. William said often that, "He was going to move back to Kansas City (at the time they lived in California) and become the biggest dope dealer in

K.C. with his cousins."

I didn't understand it at the time. And I among others tried on several occasions to convince William to change his mind and stop talking like that. We tried to encourage him to pursue basketball and college. My uncle and his wife eventually moved back to K.C. and William got his wish. As a teenager and young man, he began hanging out with his cousins and uncles that were drug dealers. Soon after that, he started dealing drugs himself. It wasn't long before William and a cousin of his became known in certain circles as upcoming high rollers by the time he was twenty-three years old. William and his cousin didn't live to see their twenty-fifth birthdays. They were gunned down and executed on the streets of Kansas City. Rumor has it that it was over a drug deal gone badly.

William thought and spoke his fate into existence. I believe in some ways, my uncle contributed to it as well. He often told William that if he didn't change his thinking and his ways he would live a short life. It became a self-fulfilling prophecy. I believe William thought he could cheat life and get rich quick with misguided intentions. It's been said time and time again, that there are no shortcuts in life. We cannot reap what we have not sown. It defies Law! Furthermore, riches are a state of mind. Wealth must first be known in the mind before it can manifest on the outside. I believe the Creator wants each and every one of us to be rich and wealthy. Not for the sake of just being wealthy and acquiring a bunch bling, bling but to spread goodwill and peace to all mankind.

According to the Kabbalist, we are to desire wealth and have stewardship over millions so that we can expand humanity with our own individual gifts and talents in the most positive way. To receive abundance just for the sake of receiving is unfulfilling but to receive for the sake of sharing, is everything. I believe this explains in part why so many famous Hollywood stars and professional sports players regardless of how much money they amass, they go broke or destroy their lives with drugs and alcohol or commit suicide. If you acquire money without Good (or God) intentions and you are not living out your life's purpose (to expand the world with your special talents unique only to you) your seeds will be planted in unfertile soil.

With our words, we can plant seeds that grow beautiful flowers or monstrous weeds. Whatever type of seeds we end up planting is the choice we make every time we open our mouth and speak. What types of seeds are you committed to planting today?

The Art of Forgiveness

There is no particular formula
or method or ideal time for forgiveness.

Forgiveness starts with a single thought,
a slight swift in ones consciousness to live,
be and think differently from the moment before.
When one changes the way he or she views an idea, a
person or thing the way we look at things will
begin to change as well.

It is in these moments that life takes on an
entire different meaning.

Forgiveness is appreciating, accepting, knowing,
And allowing yourself and others to be whom and
what they are RIGHT NOW.

In forgiveness there is no pain only Goodness.
In the knowing of Good is the knowing of God
(SOURCE).

Forgive so that you may know GOODNESS/GOD.

Author- Nnika Tinney

CHAPTER SIX

The Art of Forgiveness

Forgiveness is one of those action words that is often more easier to say then it is to put into practice. Most of us have heard the saying, "It's better to forgive and forget it". But I wonder how often this old adage is actually practiced. Considering there is always a war going in somewhere in the world since practically the beginning of time, it would be safe to say that mankind has still not mastered the vital lessons this sweet little saying has been trying to impart upon us for centuries. Why do you think that is? I am sure we could all speculate and come up with one reason or another. The truth of the matter is from my perspective is that we have challenges forgiving others because we struggle with self-forgiveness. If you can't forgive yourself when you do something that you know wasn't in your best interest so to speak and you constantly beat yourself up over it subconsciously year after year. Then how could you possibly forgive someone else outside of yourself? I've heard some say, "I forgive but I don't ever forget!" Well, I am here to break it to you that if you won't allow yourself to forget; then most certainly you won't allow your entire self to forgive either. The moment that individual or event happens again, you will bring the memory back up in your mind as your proof source to show why you should not have forgiven the person in the first place. It's a clever mind trick that we play on ourselves.

We set ourselves up to have reasons to be resentful. So we don't have to forgive. Since we do not allow ourselves to forget, we can always have an escape goat or justification to be right and an emotional obligation to our EGO self to continue to play the victim role. Did you get that? That was a mouthful. You might want to read that again. When we become upset with someone or we chose to be offended by what someone says or does it's really not the other person that is the problem. The problem is within us. I say that because we are actually more like a magnet than any other object that exists. We draw to ourselves the same people, places and situations that are in harmony with ourselves. In other words, just as the Universal Law of Attractions states, "That which is like to itself is draw to itself." Another way to put it is "You reap what you sow." If you have trouble forgiving yourself, then you will attract other people to you who exhibit some of the same habits or characteristics as you. That is law. If one of your goals in life is to live a life filled with joy and happiness, then you can't possibly do that if you won't forgive. The first step in the forgiveness process is to give you permission to forgive yourself. If in doubt, just remember and remind yourself of the old scripture saying of *"Love thy neighbor, as Thy Self."* The key words in that phrase are LOVE and SELF. Most of the time we tell ourselves that it takes a longtime to get past a major event like a divorce, the death of a love one, the loss of a job or a disagreement with a relative, friend or neighborhood. This is a lie we humans have been selling ourselves on it for centuries. Forgiveness is like falling in love. It can happen in an instant, if you are open to it.

Forgiveness starts with a single thought; a slight shift in one's consciousness to live, be and think differently from the moment before.

How do you Forgive a Parent or Caretaker whom you were Deeply Hurt By?

The art of forgiveness can be tricky sometimes. What I mean is that sometimes we may think we have forgiven someone about something just to find ourselves upset again over the same issue. A few years ago, I thought I had totally forgiven my father for ruining his life with drugs and alcohol and causing havoc on the family because of his addiction problems. But then a few years ago, he called me up and said that he wished everyone would just leave him alone and let him live his life anyway he very well pleased. At first, I became angry with him and I wanted to convince him to live a drug free life. I thought to myself, "You said you were over this, why are getting upset over his choices?" I soon realized that there was still some residual pain left over from my childhood as a result of my father's addiction problems that I hadn't forgiven yet. I immediately told myself that I love me and forgave myself and that it was ok to still love and care for my dad in spite of his choices. I was then able to express to my dad that I loved him. Regardless of what he choose to do with his life and even though I wouldn't make the same choices for mines, that he was entitled to live his life however he saw fit. I send him positive thoughts *every day.*

Forgiveness is appreciating, accepting, knowing, and allowing yourself and others to be whom and what they are **RIGHT NOW**. **In forgiveness there is no pain** *only Goodness. In the knowing of Good is the knowing of God (SOURCE). I finally forgave him so that I may know GOODNESS/GOD.*

I can say I have also released my anger and resentment for my biological mother as well. Some say for a child to forgive a mother is much more difficult than forgiving a father. Perhaps it's because the mother is the one that carries the child in her womb and gives birth to that child. I would have to disagree with that. I think it can be equally difficult depending on the child. In my case, it was the opposite because I always felt closer to my father than my birth mother for whatever reasons and so it was much easier to forgive her than him. With my mother, I was her second child she bore and with my father I was his first child. Maybe my birth order with each parent also played a factor in it. I always felt as a small child, that my father cared more for my well-being and me than my mother did.

I didn't understand why until years later when I became an adult and my mother and I had a chance to really talk woman to woman. I had always wondered why her and my father got a divorce after just a few short years of marriage from her point of view. My father had always maintained that it was because my mother cheated on him while he was incarcerated for shooting and killing a neighbor's dog that had viciously acted against one of the baby brothers. And secondly, he said that he never really was in love with my mother like they were as teenagers when they met. After she had become pregnant with me, my father's mother insisted that they get married because she didn't want any bastard grandchildren. My father was the oldest of eight children and he said it was not tolerated to go against my grandmother at the time. So out of guilt, he said he would marry her. I always say that there are three sides to a story, his side, her side and the truth.

My mother contended that they were in love and that she left my father while he was jail because he was physically abusive. She said she saw an opportunity to get out of the relationship and she took it. She said, "Even though I only had an eighth grade education, I still ain't no fool!" I can't say I can be upset with her for that. Even after he was released, she said he found out where she lived and beat her up one last time. I suppose to prove that he still had some power over her. She told me she didn't want to have another child at the time because she already had my sister whom she had given birth to at the age of fifteen. My father insisted that she not terminate her pregnancy and 40 weeks later I was born. I understood after hearing this story why I most likely felt a closer bond to my dad. He wanted me and she didn't. She communicated this to me while I was still in her womb with her thoughts! And I on a subconscious level picked up on it without even realizing it. We are such powerful co-creators that we can pollute an unborn fetus' mind with our thoughts.

After living part-time with my birth mother and part-time with my father and step mother when I was thirteen, my birth mother finally decided that smoking crack cocaine was more important to her than raising me and my two sisters. She gave each one of us to our prospective fathers for good. I use to think how a woman could give up her children especially for drugs. I am now so gratefully that she did. What she did was truly an act of love. Though my dad had his issues as well, for the most part, he and my stepmother kept a roof over our heads and food on the table. Things weren't always easy or pleasant but it was better than the alternative. Even with my dad's addiction problems, he worked very hard for over twenty years in the construction industry as a laborer and carpenter. I learned from him what it means to feel like you have to work hard to create a dollar and how Stinkin Thinkin can really create a life of turmoil, struggle and disappointments for oneself.

My stepmother, who I call my mother because she is the one that has been there for me since I was 18 months old, was a college graduate and she always encouraged me to stay in school. She played a big part as to why I had a burning desire to get into a four-year university. My cousin Danny, who was in college while I was in high school, along with some of my teachers and guidance counselors played a role in feeding my desire to obtain a college degree. I remember my sophomore year in college, calling my mom and telling her I had applied for a special program that my school along with several others had put together that gave students an opportunity to study in Washington D.C. for a quarter. I was nervous that I might not get accepted because there were a lot of students applying. The selection process was based on

GPA, a roundtable interview and writing an essay telling why you should be selected. She told me that God was on my side and that the Creator has always been on my side. She said that I had angels looking out for me and I would get into the program. She was most certainly right! Not only did I get into the program, but also I was also able to do my internship at The White House! That was a great experience for me. I got to meet a lot of powerful political people including Former President Clinton and First Lady Hillary. Though I felt at times my mother was overly strict and controlling, I am truly grateful that I had and have her in my life.

I want everyone to remember this "What you don't forgive, you will relive". I heard a gentleman say this one day while I sat in a two-day workshop and I have never forgotten it. If you find yourself not living the type of life you had imagined for yourself when you were growing up as child, ask yourself "Whom do I need to forgive?" If you consistently suffer from different physical infirmities ask yourself, "Whom do I need to forgive?" I know of someone who suffered from cancer at one point. After it was pointed out to her, that she still held tremendous resentment for her ex-husband and that she needed to let go of these harsh feelings she was harboring in order to get on the road of recovery; she made a miraculous recovery and became cancer free.

Are You Open?

Being open brings up another word for discussion. Once a friend of mine asked me, "How do I open up so that I can attract the right mate for me into my life?" Just like forgiveness or anything else in life, you have to be open to the idea of it first. To be open, simply means to let go of any preconceived ideas of how or what something is supposed to be like. One of the exercises that my business partner and I practice regularly is saying certain action-oriented affirmations of what we want our subconscious minds to do. For example, we will say something like, "I open my heart, my mind and my soul to receive ……." If you are feeling down or angry or depressed and you are not sure why, you can simply state the above affirmation and feel in the blank with whatever you want and I guarantee that feeling of dreary will leave you. Be sure you are somewhere in place or environment where you can relax and take long deep breaths in and out. The key to any affirmation exercise is in the breathing. Breathing long and deep has many physical health benefits not to mention mental ones. Which is why if you have ever had the privilege to witness a woman giving birth, the one main consistent thing that you heard the doctors and nurses say to the mother to be is to "**BREATHE.**" Whenever a woman is getting ready for a contraction or to push the baby forward through the birth canal, the medical staff tells her to take a long deep breath from her diaphragm. The medical profession has since known that our power comes from our diaphragm area (that place from your navel to just below your hips). It is that power along with the mental power from the mother that assists in bringing each and every one of us into this world. It doesn't even matter if you were born by way of cesarean. Prior to your birth, your mother still utilized the breath and her core power from her abdomen area to carry you in her womb until your birth date.

What Kinds of Things Happen When We Are Open?

When we are open, what appears like miracles, begin to happen. Although they really are not miracles, because we are part of unfaultable substance so really there is nothing that is truly impossible. We call things impossible but when a situation changes to our favor, we label them as miracles. When we are truly open, we are able to reach our goals and live out our dreams. We meet that special someone, we get that promising position, and we obtain that dream house or dream car and so on and so forth. The right people, places and things begin to show up in our lives when we are open and unattached to the outcome. When we are open and unattached; people, places or events don't have the same type of effect on us. We are not completely thrown off course when situations don't turn out like we planned. You are to look at the situation, observe it and ask yourself "What can I learn from this or what am I supposed to learn from this?"

During the real estate boom, I finally made up my mind that I wanted to acquire real estate investment properties so that I could create and build long-term wealth for my daughters and myself.

I had been given several opportunities in the past to obtain this goal but I allowed my own fears and the fear of others stop me.

Though I was going through a divorce at the time, I hired a Success Coach who encouraged me to go after my dreams of becoming a real investor. Several dear friends of mine also gave encouraging words to me to pursue my dreams. Thanks to the assistance from my coach and a dear friend of mine, my career was booming and I was making a nice six-figure income.

I said to myself "Ok this time, I am not going to let anything stop me from obtaining this goal I had set for myself." I had learned from several people that the market in Arizona was a good market to buy affordable rental properties. I was able to connect with realtor Lee Robinson, in the Phoenix through a co-worker at the time. Within in six months, I became the proud owner of four properties (well actually five, I sold one). The interesting part about the process is that during the time I was buying my properties the market was really hot and most certainly a seller's market as one would say in the real estate industry. There were multiple offers and bid wars and even waiting list on some properties. My realtor, Lee was having a challenge getting offers accepted on behalf of his clients. He had placed an offer on my behalf for properties with several thousand dollars above the asking price. Lee called me one day, I remember this call like it was yesterday and said, "You are not going to believe this, but one of the properties you put in for has a counter offer from the seller on it." I said, "A counter offer, ok what does it say?" He said, "The sellers don't want you to over pay for the house. They said if we rewrite the offer and lower our offering price down to their asking price, they will accept your offer". He then went on to say, "I have other clients whom I can't get offer's accepted for, but here you are with a seller who is asking you to lower your offer price. You have to be one of the luckiest women in the world!" Yes, that's correct folks. This is a true story. This really did happen to me. Actually, it happened to me twice. How do you explain that? All I can say is that I was indeed open but I wasn't attached to the outcome. I knew I would be successful in this endeavor and I was.

Owning rental properties wasn't easy. I have had several tenants over the years break their lease and move out without notice. Leave trash and dog fescues throughout the house. I had one who even took the plants out of the front yard! Talk about Stinkin Thinkin! I have also had several people tell me that it would be advantageous for me to acquire more patience with others and myself. Several of my coaches told me that once I got the lesson these tenants came to teach me; then I would start attracting better, more responsible tenants. So true oh so true. I had a tenant who has rented from me for over a year who recently called me and said that she was giving her thirty-day notice and was moving out of the area. She has since referred me three potential tenants and has taken it upon herself to show the property to these individuals.

I am really thankful to her for that. And I pray that I have learned my lessons. (Smile) Although the real market imploded I wouldn't change that experience for nothing in the world.

The next time you find yourself upset over something or someone, stop and ask yourself "Am I breathing normally?" Step outside of your physical body, so to speak and watch yourself. Watch your breathing, watch your posture, and watch your thoughts and most of all watch your words. If you start doing this, I guarantee you that you will find yourself getting upset less often. I know that whenever I do this, I crack myself up because I see myself how others must see and sometimes it's a downright comedy show. It truly pays to be, open, unattached and to learn the lesson in more ways than one.

The Ultimate Secret

*I know that there is only One Ultimate source
from which all Creativity stems.*

*I realize there can be no Separation in this source
from My creative Mind.*

*Therefore, my mind creativity is part of
The Ultimate source of Creativity.*

The Ultimate Secret, is in my spoken word and when

I speak my desires, express my intent and know That

it is when this Ultimate Secret Source is activated.

I am convinced my word has power.

*I know that this Source is really no Secret but that the
answer to this so-called mystery is in the lack of self-
awareness.*

*I firmly believe this and I now speak my Word of em-
powerment, I let go and I allow this Ultimate Secret
To work through me.*

*No past transgressions can halt or suppress me. Pro-
crastination and self-sabotage do not exist in my life,*

Time is irrelevant to this Ultimate source of ALL THINGS, and I therefore know and Expect the best right now.

I'm willing to let go of anything or anyone that hinders my true-life purpose.

I am inspired or in spirit to act upon every increasing opportunity to live out my true destiny.

And so it is.

Author- Nnika Tinney

CHAPTER SEVEN

Know They Self

<u>Live A Life That Matters</u>

Ready or not, some day it will all come to an end.

There will be no more sunrises, no minutes, hours or days. All the things you collected, whether treasured or forgotten, will pass to someone else.
Your wealth, fame and temporal power will shrivel to irrelevance. Your grudges, resentments, frustrations, and jealousies will finally disappear.
So, too, your hopes, ambitions, plans, and to-do lists will expire. The wins and losses that once seemed so important will fade away. It won't matter where you came from, or on what side of the tracks you lived, at the end. It won't matter whether you were beautiful or

brilliant. Even your gender and skin color will be irrelevant. So what will matter? How will the value of your days be measured?

What will matter is not what you bought, but what you built; not what you got, but what you gave. What will matter is not your success, but your significance. What will matter is not what you learned, but what you taught.

What will matter is every act of integrity, compassion, courage or sacrifice that enriched, empowered or encouraged others to emulate your example. What will matter is not your competence, but your character. What will matter is not how many people you knew, but how many will feel a lasting loss when you're gone. What will matter is not your memories, but the memories that live in those who loved you. What will matter is how long you will be remembered, by whom and for what.

Living a life that matters doesn't happen by accident. It's not a matter of circumstance but of choice. Choose to live a life that matters.

Author Unknown

Ｗhat does it mean to, "Know Thy Self?" We heard this saying many times and read it in ancient scriptures, but have we really taken the time to learn and understand what the writer really meant when he/she wrote these words? Like most people, I have just begun to know myself. Don't get me wrong, for years I thought I knew who I was. It wasn't until in the last few years have I realized that the person I thought I was or was supposed to be wasn't the real me. Let me explain. You see like many of you; I grew with this idea of what I was based on what I had been taught by my parents, teachers, society, etc. I thought I was a black female, born into a dysfunctional family infested with drugs, alcohol, domestic violence, criminal activity mixed in with some good old fashion Baptist religion to boot! I thought I was this underprivileged kid, who in spite of all the pitfalls overcame all of that stuff to become a product member of society. Although that is all true, it's still not who I am. You see after much soul searching and deep meditation, I realized that I am much more than any title given to me and that I choose to accept myself. What I realized is that when I stripped away all the titles of being black, a female, underprivileged, divorced, working class professional, college graduate, homeowner, etc. I was left with a unique individual who came to this earth plain with a purpose. I realized that I am a soul full of spirit and life. When we take away all the titles, the material possessions and even the people we surround ourselves with we are left with our oneness. When we get quiet to ourselves, we then can begin to really hear the Spirit inside of us speak.

Hate to Be Alone

If you are at all like me, you dread being alone. Although, I am getting more use to the idea every day. I grew up in house with three other siblings and so there was always someone around. I didn't realize it until I became an adult that I didn't like to be in the house alone for any long period of time. My life coach pointed out to me not long ago, that I was still holding onto this childhood fear of being alone. That was one of the reasons why I was settling for relationships that were less than what I deserved. I realized with her assistance, that I am never really alone because Spirit is always with me. When you can get to a place where you recognize this, you know that you are on the path of "Knowing Thy Self." To know yourself is to

Know That the Creator of All Things Dwells within You!

We are a product of our Creator and therefore a piece of this force, this Power must also reside within each and every one of us. If that is true, is it possible for us to ever really be alone? I would have to say no.

The Best Person to Love

If you haven't guessed by now, the best person to love is you! There will be no one like you nor has there ever been anyone exactly like you. So why not fall in love with yourself? You are probably the most self-critical and stubborn person that you have ever met. If you master loving yourself, then loving someone else regardless of their shortcomings will be a cinch. This I believe is the key to experiencing true love with another person. Many times we will experience challenging relationships with others because we have not mastered how to love ourselves. It's easy to spot people who are truly in love with themselves and recognize their own self-value. They tend to have a genuine love and respect for others as well. The same can be said for people who are self-loafing, insincere and have low self-esteem. People that haven't learned to love themselves often times have a hard time with loving others, commitment, are self- destructive and play small in life. When you lack self-love, you allow anything or anyone to steer you away from living out your life purpose or discovering your life purpose. However when you truly wake-up and love yourself, you understand that living out your life purpose and expanding humanity with your special gift is all there is and nothing can detour you. Does that mean you don't get knocked down sometimes? You do. However someone that is truly consciously aware of self and the Creator within, knows how to quickly regain their composure and get back on the road of living life. Are you living your life or is life living you?

Create Your Own Expectation and Do What You Can to Live Up to Those

I feel many times, self-hatred and self-criticism stems from trying to live up to someone else's expectations of what we should be. There is no judgment here. This is just simply an observation I have made about myself and others I have come into contact with. As we grow and develop as children; our parents, caregivers, teachers, preacher, etc. create expectations for us. Even before our mothers deliver us; our parents, relatives, etc. sit around and discuss what you are going to be when you grow up. In some cultures it's already pre-determined; who you are going to marry, where you going to live, and what career you are to have. If we are not mindful, we fall into this trap and grow up trying to live up to others expectations and dreams instead of pursuing our own individual dreams. I don't feel I was really ever pressured to pursue a certain career. However there was this unspoken vibe that I'd better grow up and be successful. Not so much because it's good to a successful, productive and contributing member of society but more so to prove to others that my father and mother and their parents didn't produce all dysfunctional offspring. I don't blame anyone for this. As a matter of fact, I placed much of this pressure on myself. I spent a huge part of life trying to prove that I could do much better than my parents no matter what it took even if I got off course (which I did do a few times).

If you live your life based on someone else's expectations, you will always have something to prove. My partner and I always say, "Whenever you are seeking someone's approval, you become their slave." In my case it didn't matter how successful materially I became and how much I gave to my family, it was expected that I give more.

Don't get me wrong; I don't have a problem with giving. Giving is just as important as receiving. They are equal in my book. Certain members of my family would make comments to me like, "God blessed you so much so, that you could be in this position to give." I think that this statement does have some truth in it. However, I don't believe that it is my responsibility to financially support individuals that are not completely willing to help themselves. I think it is unproductive and not planting your seeds in good soil if you continue to give someone money, for instance and they don't take inspired (spiritually guided) actions to change their circumstances for the better in a fruitful way. When we do this we are not helping those individuals, we are actually hindering them and contributing to prolonging their lessons. I believe that we all are faced with trials and tribulations to teach us a lesson so that we can grow and manifest all the Goodness in us to the world. Once you have learned the lesson, the trials will disappear. Since the Universe is constantly changing and expanding, new lessons will appear. But without them where would we be? Life would be boring. So let's embrace the lessons, see them as opportunities to create magic in our lives and the lives of others. Besides, if the Creator blesses me, Oprah, Mark Cuban or anyone else for that matter, then the Creator will most certainly do the same for you! That's one check (a check is a promise to pay) you can take to the bank and cash confidently because its sources are limitless. If we are to live happy and fulfilling lives than we must be of clear mind, have good intentions, speak words of abundance and prosperity and create our own expectations for ourselves.

"Our deepest fear is not that we are inadequate. Our deepest fear is that we are powerful measure. It is our Light, not our Darkness, that most frightens us.

We ask ourselves, who am I to be brilliant, gorgeous, talented, and fabulous?

Actually, who are you NOT to be?

You are a child of God.

Your playing small does not serve the World.

There is nothing enlightened about shrinking so that other people won't feel insecure around you.

We were born to make manifest the glory of God that is within us.

It is not just in some of us; it is in everyone.

As we let our own light shine, we unconsciously give other People permission to do the same.

As we are liberated from our own fear, our presence Automatically liberates others."

Author- **Marianne Williamson**

CHAPTER EIGHT

The True Meaning of a Diva

Society has coined the phrase DIVA to mean all sorts of things. Mainly a woman with much attitude who when she walks into a room she commands attention with her presence, looks, and tone of voice. The Webster's meaning of the word Diva is defined as a distinguished female opera singer or prima donna. I have given the term DIVA a new meaning. My definition of the word Diva means someone who has recognized and accepted the Divine, Intuitive, Valuable, Asset that they truly are. We are all divine intuitive valuable assets; the only sag is that most of us don't know this yet. The good news is that once you recognize and realize that you too are a DIVA, you begin to speak what you truly feel and you allow yourself to be vulnerable so that you have the opportunity to experience all that the Creator has in store for you. A true Diva knows how to drop drama that does not serve her. She knows what she wants and why she wants it. She doesn't waste time or preoccupy her mind with all the hows. She leaves the how, when, and where up to the Supreme Life Force. A true Diva does not allow herself to be overrun with her emotions or anyone else's emotions for that matter. A true Diva understands that she is a co-creator of her world and that her words have the Power to Inspire and to Destroy. A true Diva not only believes but she knows that no one can stop or prevent her good in spite of their best efforts.

It can be a challenge at times to look past other people when they transgress against us. However, have you ever stopped to think or ask yourself is it worth your peace of mind to harbor ill feelings toward another human being? I have tried to live my life with the principle belief that at all cost, my happiness comes first. My attitude is this, "If certain feelings are going to hinder my ability to be happy, then I must drop those feelings as soon as possible because being happy is the only way to be. As long as something is an "I should do this" or "I would like to be able to do that" than in all likelihood you won't do it until it becomes a "Must do that I choose to." It is my motto that I must be happy in whatever it is that I am doing or interacting with because there is no other way to be.

I remember approximately fifteen years ago or so; I got a call from my older sister crying that she and her kids were living place to place because she and her husband had broken up and she couldn't afford the rent on her own. I immediately jumped into action and drove over 60 miles to pick her and her kids up and moved them into my home. I talked it over with my spouse at the time and it just seemed like the right thing to do since we had a five-bedroom house and two little girls. I rented a moving truck, took her belongings out of storage because she couldn't afford the monthly storage bill and moved her things into my garage. What I didn't realize was that my sister had developed a drinking habit and suffered from extreme negative self-talk and mild depression. I assisted her with writing resumes, getting her driver's license back that she had lost due to a DUI, a job, an apartment and a car. Plus I made sure that she and her kids had plenty of food the first month they were in their apartment. To my dismay, I couldn't do enough to assist my sister no matter how hard I tried. She ultimately resented me for stepping in to assist her and fell back into her negative drinking patterns. I was hurt and angered by her lack of appreciation but I eventually understood that holding onto those feelings toward my sister would do her no good and certainly couldn't serve me. One thing is for certain that we must accept and that is regardless of our best intentions, we can't force someone to recognize the DIVA in him or her if they are not open and ready for it. Though I haven't seen my sister in a number of years, I think of her from time to time and I do wish her well. The best way I have found to help someone like my sister is to be a living example. We can demonstrate with our own life and actions the necessity for developing high Self-esteem and the vital role that the mantra of "Knowing thyself" and "Loving thyself" plays.

You see no matter what I say or what anyone else might say, nothing in your life will not change unless you accept that you are truly unique and valuable and have all the tools you need inside of you to change your life. You have been blessed with a certain gift that must be shared to expand the world. I can sit here and tell you until I am blue in the face that you are divine, intuitive and a valuable asset but until you accept that as your truth, life will not change for you.

Are you committed to yourself enough that you will hang in there long enough to reap the rewards of your labor? I can't answer that for you. Only you can answer that for yourself. I am not always sure how things are going to turn out or why things happen the way they do. Just as I am sure you probably have felt that way at times. One thing that I can say for sure is that things haven't always turned out the way I thought they should, but they have always turned out in the best way for my higher good. I am learning to embrace the little child in me more and more each day and I have to tell you it sure feels good!

CONCLUSION

Glass of Milk

One day, a poor boy who was selling goods from door to door to pay his way through school, found he had only one thin dime left, and he was hungry.

He decided he would ask for a meal at the next house.

However, he lost his nerve when a lovely young woman opened the door.

Instead of a meal he asked for a drink of water.

She thought he looked hungry so brought him a large glass of milk. He drank it so slowly, and then asked, "How much do I owe you?" "You don't owe me any-thing," she replied. "Mother has taught us never to accept pay for a kindness."

*He said, "Then I thank you from the
bottom of my heart."*

*As Howard Kelly left that house, he not only felt
stronger physically, but his faith in God and
man was strong also.*

He had been ready to give up and quit.

*Many years later that same young woman became
critically ill. The local doctors were baffled. They finally sent her to the big city, where they called in spe-
cialists to study her rare disease.*

*Dr. Howard Kelly was called in for the consultation.
When he heard the name of the town she came
from, a strange light filled his eyes.*

*Immediately he rose and went down the hall
of the hospital to her room.
Dressed in his doctor's gown he went in to see her.
He recognized her at once.
He went back to the consultation room determined
to do his best to save her life.
From that day he gave special attention to her case.*

After a long struggle, the battle was won.

Dr. Kelly requested the business office to pass the final bill to him for approval.

He looked at it, and then wrote something on the edge and the bill was sent to her room.

She feared to open it, for she was sure it would take the rest of her life to pay for it all.

Finally she looked, and something caught her attention on the side of the bill.

She read these WORDS, "Paid in full with one glass of milk"

(Signed) Dr. Howard Kelly.

Tears of joy flooded her eyes as her happy heart prayed: "Thank You God, that your love has spread broad through human hearts and hands."
There's a saying, which goes something like this:
Bread cast on the waters comes back to you.

The good deed you do today may benefit you or someone you love at the least expected time.
If you never see the deed again at least you will have made the world a better place - And, after all, isn't that what life is all about?

Now you have two choices.

You can send this book on and spread a positive message.
2. Or ignore it and pretend it never touched your heart The hardest thing to learn in life is which bridge to cross and which - To burn

Author- Unknown

I believe life sometimes is like a glass of milk (almond, I don't advocate drinking cow's milk). Sometimes it's like chocolate milk, tasty and full of flavor. And other times it's plain, but yet somehow it still manages to quench your thirst. The taste may not always be good but an Oreo cookie goes down better with a glass of milk. I decided to be thankful for my trials and celebrate the good times. And ask myself," What am I to learn from this person or situation?" Without variety in our life, where would we be? We would be no different than our pets, or favorite feline friends. Have you ever seen a worried dog or cat? No, because animals "JUST BE". They don't worry about bills, or car notes and house payments. They don't even worry about what they are going to eat because instinctively they know their needs are going to be met. They take one day at a time as it comes. Their minds aren't clouded with negative, disempowering thoughts. They don't speak words of lack, loss or limitation. If it weren't for the complexities of human behavior then I would have no cause for writing this book. So on that note, I am grateful that we can and do experience an array of emotions and thoughts. I want to leave you with this one thought and that is "Is Your Thinkin, Still Stinkin?" I hope it has improved just a little since you have read my book.

I want to challenge you to drop one disempowering thought a week. Or if you find yourself saying a certain phrase or word to yourself on a regular basis that is not positive, I challenge to stop using that word. Every time you find yourself using that word or phrase, put a dollar in a jar. Then at the end of the month, take all the money that you have put in the jar and tithe it to a spiritual organization of your choice that is assisting you. By doing this, you are planting your seeds (your words, deeds and energy) in fertile soil. In due season, you will reap a plentiful harvest. In that harvest, you find new mountains of prosperity waiting and available for you. All you have to do is claim it!

ABOUT THE AUTHOR

Nnika Tinney Wealth Strategist
Prosperous With All Odds

Nnika Tinney comes to you with over twenty years of successful marketing/sales/customer service experience, coupled with excellent educational credentials and professional accomplishments. Following a period of prudent introspection, Nnika has come to the inescapable conclusion that she has a strong obligation to her capabilities and must, at this critical juncture in her personal and professional career make an intelligent choice by sharing her unique prospective, trials and successes to a broad audience to make a stronger impact on mankind.

Having beat the odds as a child of; poverty, domestic violence, drug and alcohol abuse by both parents and the first to attend college she is able to understand people's feelings and is driven to make a difference in others. She is warm, compassionate, and friendly. Nnika is in tuned to others and she can often times anticipate other's needs–especially emotional ones.

Nnika is articulate, vivacious, enthusiastic, and an excellent public speaker because she possesses an innate sense of what her audience wants. Gifted with rarity to make personal connections, she is a skillful communicator, and prides herself on being able to tell it like it IS, all while making people feel good.

Her credentials include a string of top performances in sales and management for companies like Target Stores, Norwest Financial Services, The MoneyStore, World Savings Bank, & the State of Nevada Dept of Welfare and Housing Division. It should also be dually noted that she served her country as an Intern at the

White House, fall of 1993 during the Clinton administration. She worked directly under the supervision of Alexis Herman, Director of the Office of Public Liaison. While at the White House she participated in telephone campaign strategies by soliciting the support of major political players & presidents of large Fortune 500 and 100 companies successfully.

Nnika received her **Bachelor of Science Degree in Management and Economics** from the highly ranked University of California, at Davis and **her Master's Degree** from Bellevue University in **Public Administration**. She is currently licensed in insurance, is Commercial Loan Specialist with the Federal Government, and is actively pursuing entrepreneurial opportunities in her spare time. Nnika is an avid learner and student of life.

Nnika has conducted numerous live and webinar sales training classes for companies like Charter Funding, Brookstone Financial Services, Wonder Agents, Discount Home Mortgage, Bayside Mortgage and Properties, Evergreen Mortgage, Supreme Lending, Primary Residential Home Loans, The Mortgage Store, to name a few. She has on several occasions been a guest lecturer at Merritt College in Oakland, California, where she led discussions on mortgage sales and financing to audiences of over 75 students. The passion she brings & the high level of professionalism that she possesses carries over to every client she works with. A Long-term care Medicaid Case Manager for nearly 3yrs where it wasn't uncommon for her to manage 800 plus cases at a time! She has done loss mitigation, foreclosure prevention & mortgage loan modification work. She's has been a panelist speaker on FDIC sponsored events, Women's Council of Realtors events, & the National Association of Hispanics Professionals to name a few. Nnika was also the State of Nevada Home-buyer Down- payment Assistance Program Officer for over four years where she helped over 10,000 Nevada families obtain homeownership.

She also taught and trained loan officers, realtors, and the community at large on various down-payment assistance programs and mortgage tax credit programs. She has been recognized by the National Educators Council for her work in the Financial Literacy Movement-April, 2017. Nnika's agency Cromwell Financial & Insurance were proud members of The Las Vegas Urban Chamber of Commerce, The Las Vegas National Association of Real Estate Brokers, & The Las Vegas Women's Chamber of Commerce. In addition to providing financial services and estate planning products to her client, Nnika conducts workshops on Financial Literacy such as Learn to Live Debt-Free & Truly Wealthy, Foreclosure Prevention & Mortgage Protection What Your Banker Doesn't Want You to Know, How to Buy A Home With Little to No Money Out of Pocket, Maximize Your SSA Benefits By Planning Ahead, Create a 5- Figure Tax-Free Retirement Plan on a $50,000/year Income Nnika's, "Six Hours, To Six Figures Sales & Marketing Bootcamp", for Real Estate Professionals. So many tips and value given Realtors Just Can't Get Enough!

Nnika teaches financial strategist that allow families and individuals to Live Debt- free & truly Wealthy. Nnika is **The Wealth Strategist**, prospering with all odds. She is dedicated to assisting others in elevating their level of prosperity, "One Life at a Time." To learn more about the products and services that Nnika offers please visit her at www.west-coast-media-solutions.com. You can also connect with her on social media

facebook.com/nnikatinney

linkedin/com/n/nnikatinney

nnikasjourneytofinancialfreedom

9 798681 463726